I0472280

Holy Spirit Meditation Drawings
A Coloring Book For Everyone
by Nathan Jalani Taylor

#1

COLORING TIPS

1 Use color pencils, crayons, pastels, pens or markers. Also, experiment with other materials.

2 Use the blank space on the last page of this book to test different mediums.

3 To protect your pages from indents and bleed through, slip in a couple sheets of blank paper behind the page that you are coloring.

4 mix colors and blend for shading and lighting effects.

5 You don't have to stay inside the lines.

6 Print out these pages for free online. Select "centered" and "scale to fit" in page setup.

7 Take your time, have fun and enjoy!

© 2016. Nathan Jalani Taylor
www.nathanjalanitaylor.com

Man Going The One's Way

The way of the one,
the truth and the life.
Walker of the Way.
Keeper of the Code.
Honorer of the Ancestors.
Seeker of the Truth.
The path is not easy.
However, not a burden.
In fact, there can be no freedom
without discipline.
Led by the Holy Spirit
on the straight way.
Passionate lover of what is good.
Salutations to the goodhearted.
Light as a feather.
although Imperfect, flawed with scars,
stumbles along the way
but never will he fall off
by God's grace.
Humble in his wisdom and knowledge,
teacher of what is right.
Gentleness kindness and patience.
Beautiful in spirit,
shine bright like black diamonds.
Joy and sorrow on the road of the one
with purpose and glory.
- nathanjtaylor

"In the path of righteousness is life,
and in its pathway there is no death."
-Proverbs 12:28

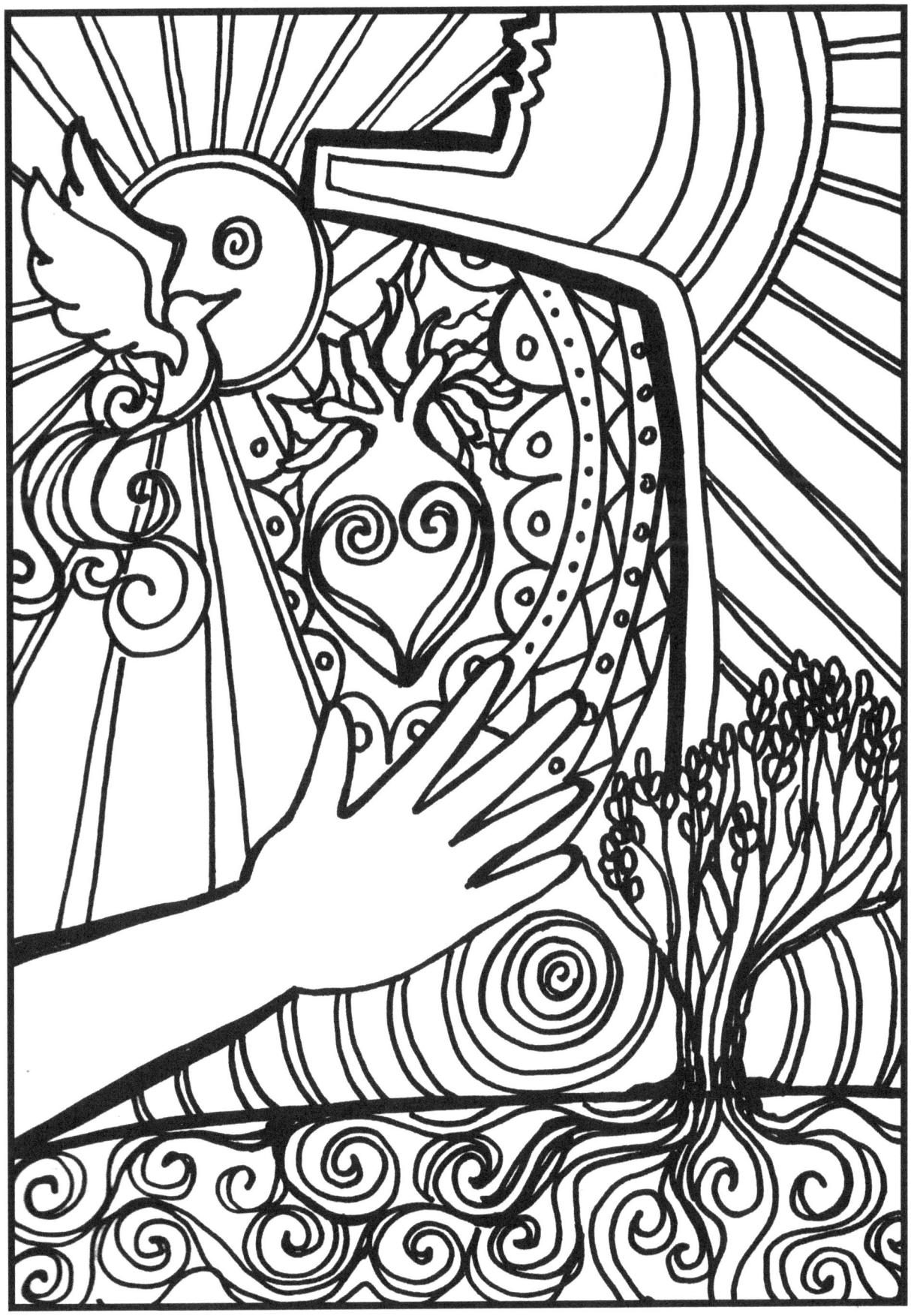

"And you shall know the truth, and the truth shall make you free."

-Jesus

HOLY SPIRIT MEDITATION DRAWINGS DEFINITION & ETYMOLOGY

holy (adj.): Old English halig "holy, consecrated, sacred; godly; ecclesiastical," from Proto-Germanic *hailaga- (source also of Old Norse heilagr, Danish hellig, Old Frisian helich "holy," Old Saxon helag, Middle Dutch helich, Old High German heilag, German heilig, Gothic hailags "holy"), from PIE *kailo- "whole, uninjured" (see health). Adopted at conversion for Latin sanctus.

spirit (n.): mid-13c., "animating or vital principle in man and animals," from Anglo-French spirit, Old French espirit "spirit, soul" (12c., Modern French esprit) and directly from Latin spiritus "a breathing (respiration, and of the wind), breath; breath of a god," hence "inspiration; breath of life," hence "life;" also "disposition, character; high spirit, vigor, courage; pride, arrogance," related to spirare "to breathe," perhaps from PIE *(s)peis- "to blow"

meditation (n.): c. 1200, "contemplation; devout preoccupation; devotions, prayer," from Old French meditacion "thought, reflection, study," and directly from Latin meditationem (nominative meditatio) "a thinking over, meditation," noun of action from past participle stem of meditari "to meditate, think over, reflect, consider," frequentative form from PIE root *med- "to measure, limit, consider, advise, take appropriate measures" (source also of Greek medesthai "think about," medon "ruler;" Latin modus "measure, manner," modestus "moderate," modernus "modern," mederi "to heal," medicus "physician;" Sanskrit midiur "I judge, estimate;" Welsh meddwl "mind, thinking;" Gothic miton, Old English metan "to measure;" also see medical).

drawing (n.): c. 1300, "a pulling," in various senses, verbal noun from draw (v.). The "picture-making" sense is from 1520s; of the picture itself from 1660s. Drawing board is from 1725; used in figurative expression from mid-20c. a picture, image, etc., that is made by making lines on a surface with a pencil, pen, marker, chalk, etc.,

source: www.etymonline.com

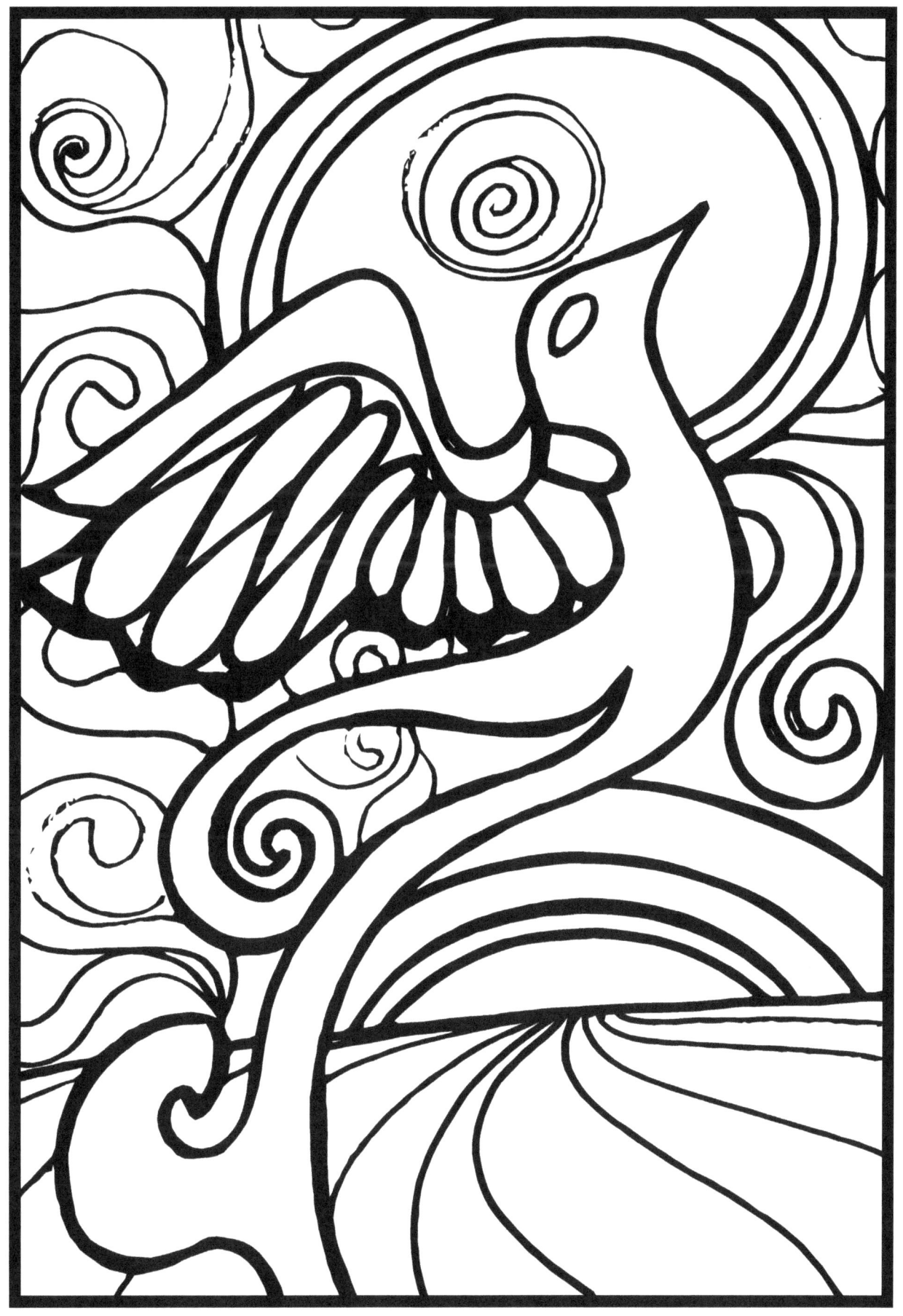

God's Grace

Who are you to say God will fail?

Have you placed the trillions of stars in the sky that properly align.
Have you laid the thousands of miles of veins that sprout from your heart.
Have you caused the birds to sing at a perfect pitch and the trees to grow.

Who are you to say God will fail?

Have you laid the foundation of your dimensional plane.
Have you designated every moment of time and space.
Have you created the elements that compose your reality.

Who are you to say God will fail?

Have you placed the billions of neurons in your brain.
Have you programmed the unlimited consciousness of your mind.
Have you engineered the atoms to vibrate in its correct frequency.

Who are you to say God will fail?

What makes you think you are anything less than amazing.
What makes you think anything is impossible with me.
I am the I am, and I invented you to love and live.

I do not fail.

A poem by Nathan Jalani Taylor
1/11/16
(inspired by Job: 38)

The Meditation Of My Heart

"Let the words of my mouth, and the meditation of my heart, be acceptable in thy sight, O Lord, my strength, and my redeemer." Psalm 19:14 (KJV)

Keywords: heart, earth, hearth, meditation, love, forgiveness, humbleness and good vibes

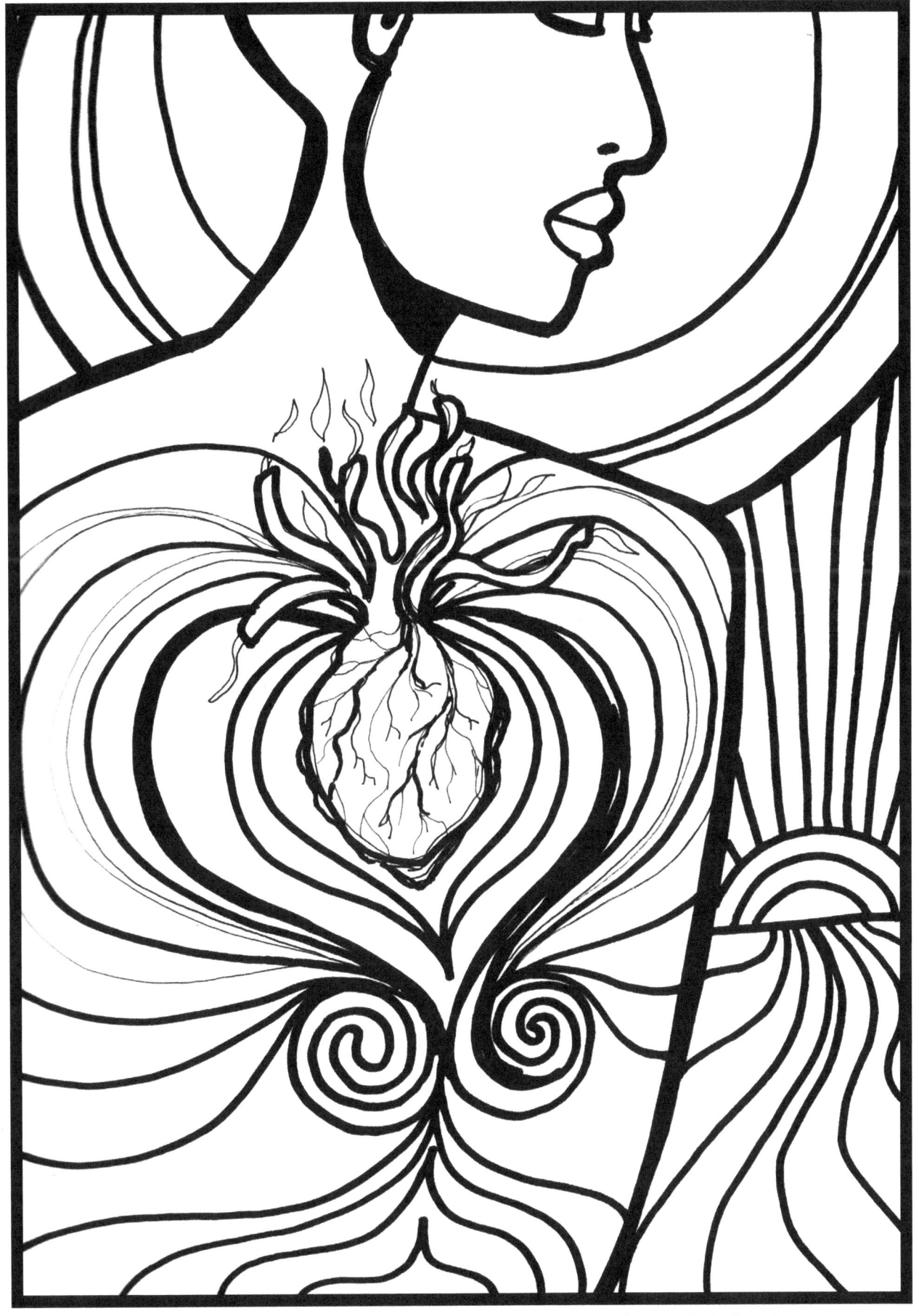

Fruit of the Holy Spirit is love, joy, peace, forbearance, kindness, goodness, faithfulness, gentleness and self-control."

Galatians 5:22-23 (NIV)

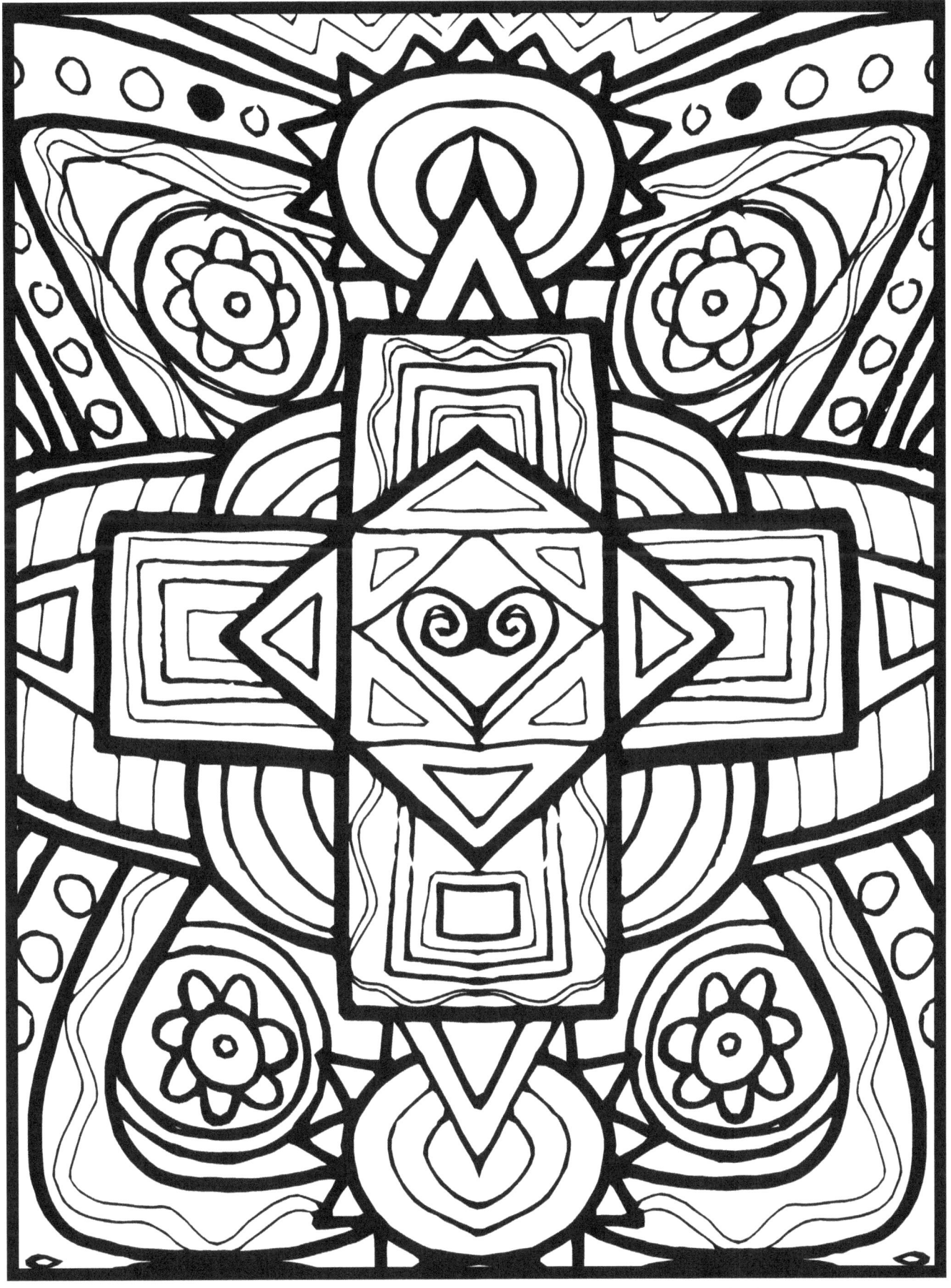

Saints Army
The Works of a Soldier of Mercy

1. Feed the hungry.

2. Give drink to the thirsty.

3. Clothe the naked.

4. Shelter the homeless

5. Visit the sick.

6. Visit the imprisoned.

7. Bury the dead.

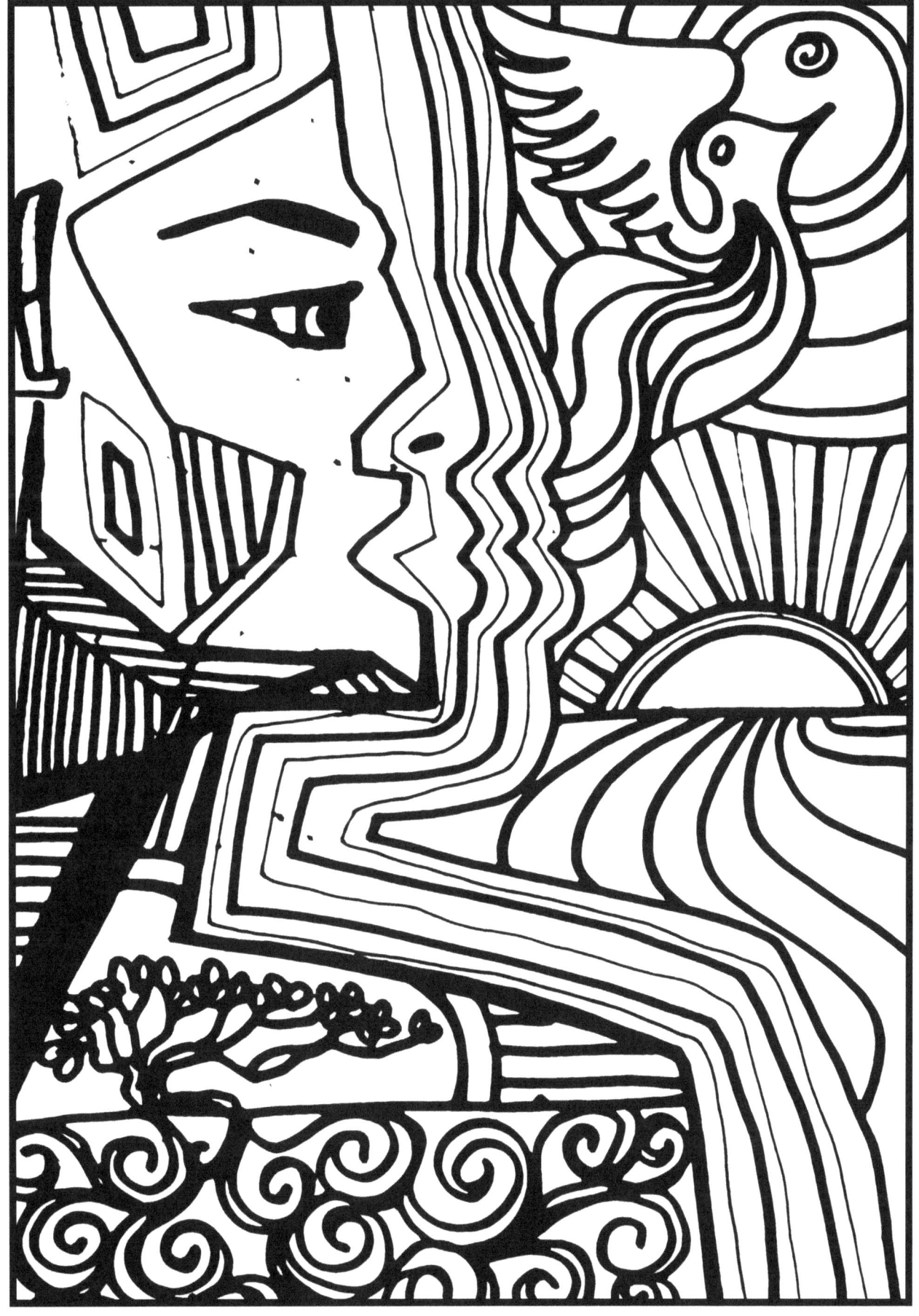

"The Spirit of the Lord is upon Me (the Messiah), Because He has anointed Me to preach the good news to the poor. He has sent Me to announce release (pardon, forgiveness) to the captives, And recovery of sight to the blind, To set free those who are oppressed (downtrodden, bruised, crushed by tragedy)

Luke 4:18 Amplified

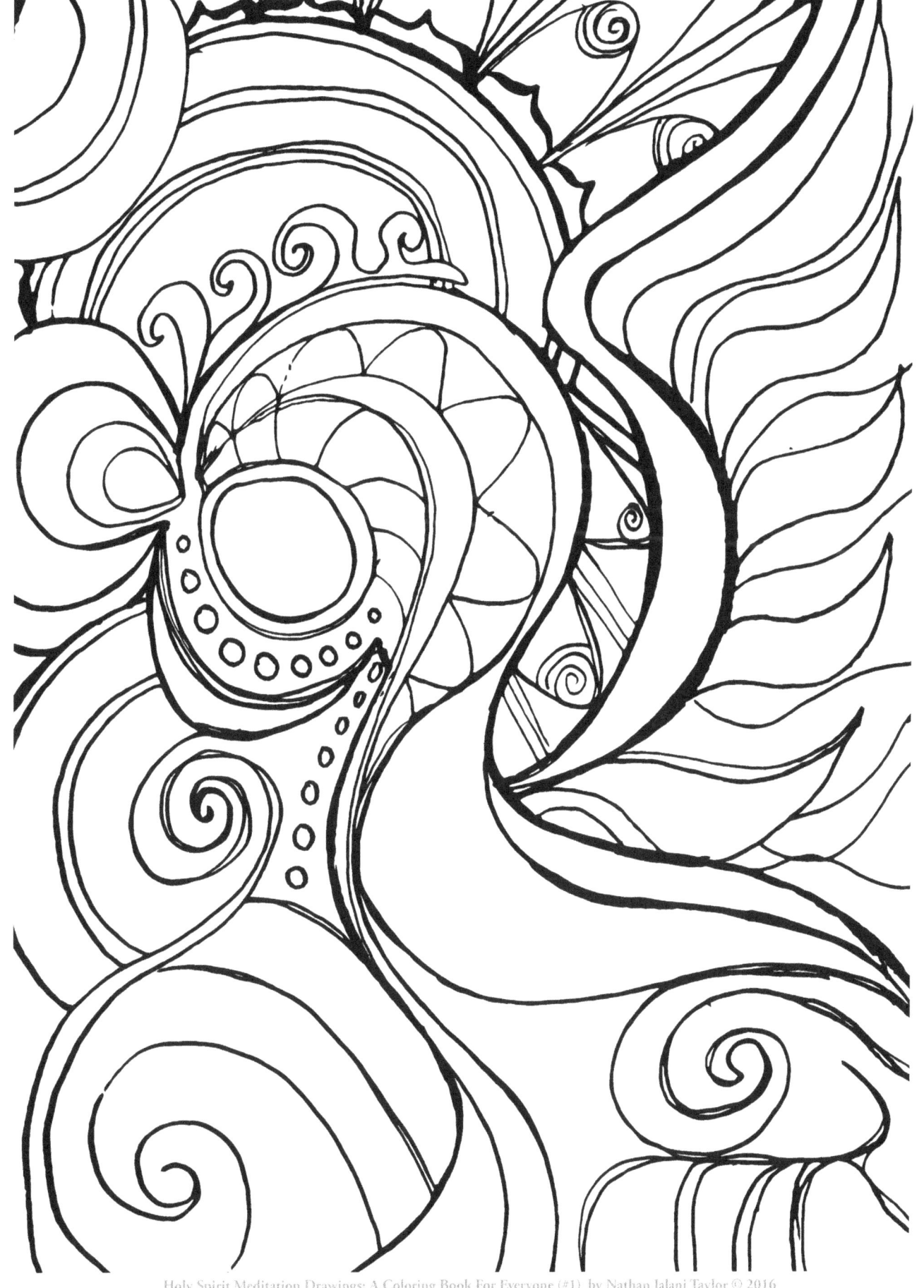

Spiritual Warrior

Finally, my brethren, be strong in the Lord, and in the power of his might. Put on the whole armor of God, that ye may be able to stand against the wiles of the devil. For we wrestle not against flesh and blood, but against principalities, against powers, against the rulers of the darkness of this world, against spiritual wickedness in high places. Wherefore take unto you the whole armor of God, that ye may be able to withstand in the evil day, and having done all, to stand. Stand therefore, having your loins girt about with truth, and having on the breastplate of righteousness; And your feet shod with the preparation of the gospel of peace; Above all, taking the shield of faith, wherewith ye shall be able to quench all the fiery darts of the wicked. And take the helmet of salvation, and the sword of the Spirit, which is the word of God: Praying always with all prayer and supplication in the Spirit, and watching thereunto with all perseverance and supplication for all saints. ***Ephesians 6:10-18***

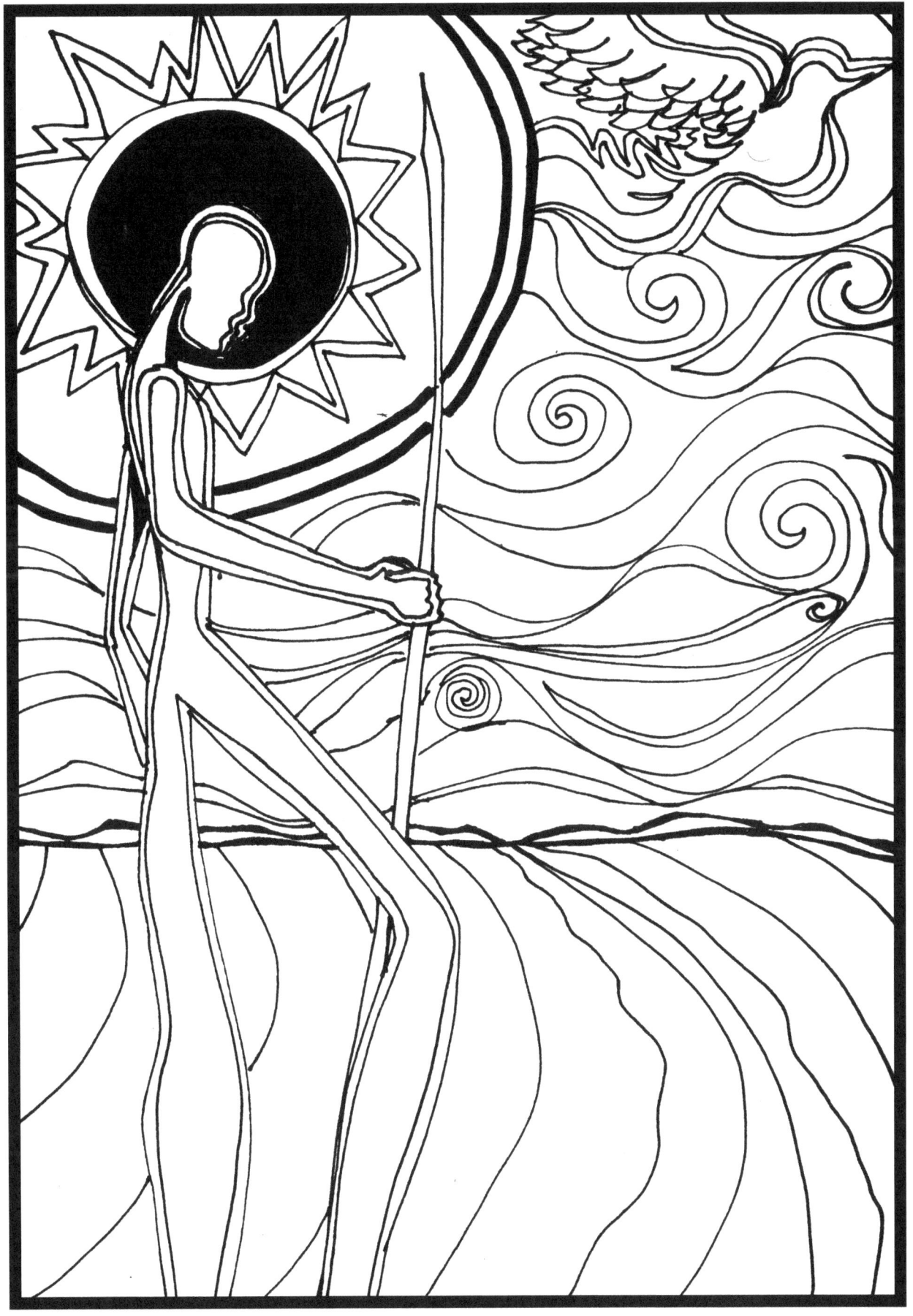

For God has not given us the spirit of fear; but of power, and of love, and of a sound mind.

2 Timothy 1:7 (AKJV)

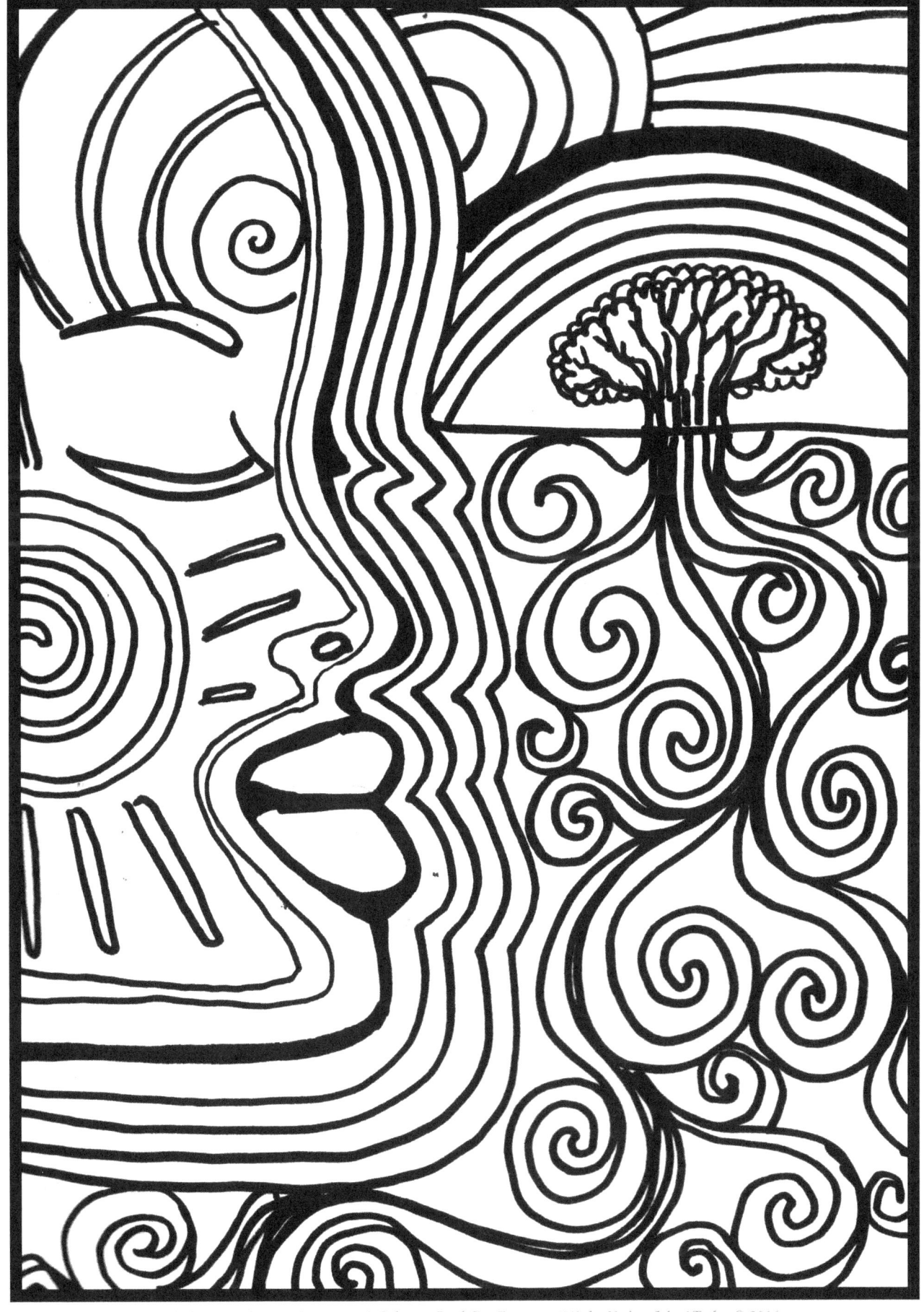

T hen Jesus cried out and said, "He who believes in Me, believes not in Me but in Him who sent Me. And he who sees Me sees Him who sent Me. I have come as a light into the world, that whoever believes in Me should not abide in darkness. And if anyone hears My words and does not believe, I do not judge him; for I did not come to judge the world but to save the world. He who rejects Me, and does not receive My words, has that which judges him—the word that I have spoken will judge him in the last day. For I have not spoken on My own authority; but the Father who sent Me gave Me a command, what I should say and what I should speak. And I know that His command is everlasting life. Therefore, whatever I speak, just as the Father has told Me, so I speak." *John 12:44-50*

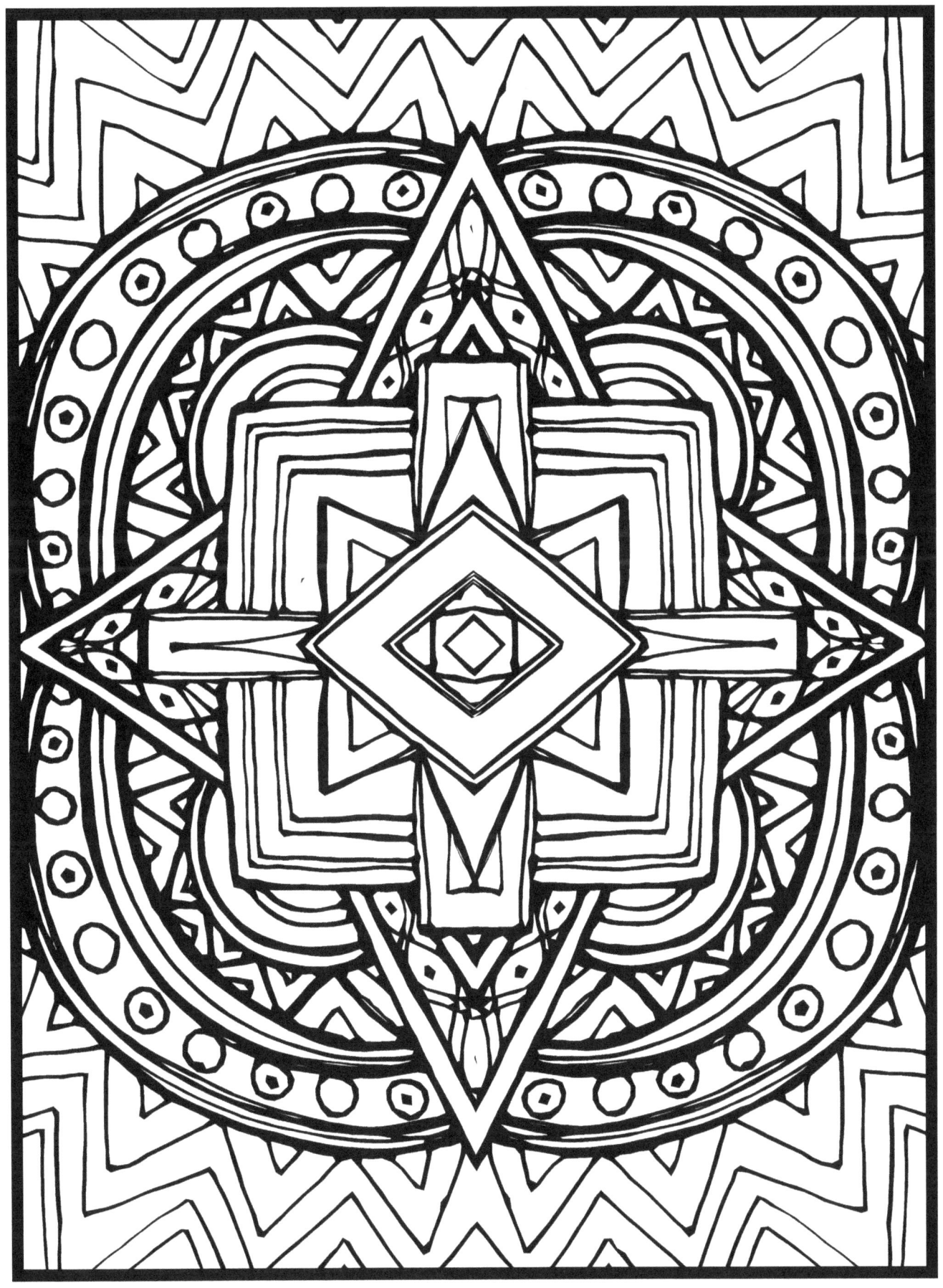

"I tell you, stop being worried or anxious (perpetually uneasy, distracted) about your life, as to what you will eat or what you will drink; nor about your body, as to what you will wear. Is life not more than food, and the body more than clothing? Look at the birds of the air; they neither sow seed nor reap the harvest nor gather the crops into barns, and yet your heavenly Father keeps feeding them. Are you not worth much more than they? And who of you by worrying can add one hour to the length of his life?" -Jesus

Matthew 5:25-27 (amplified)

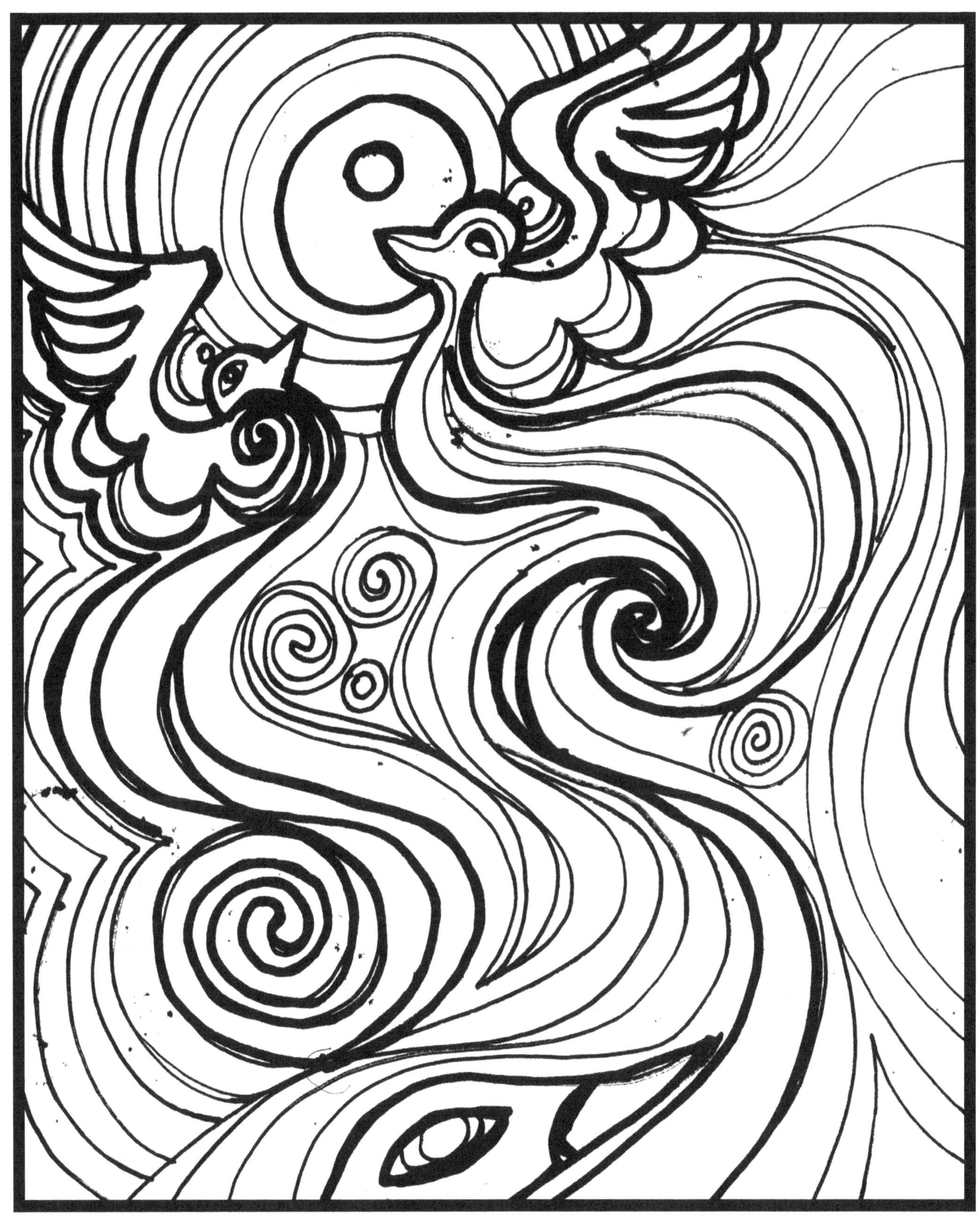

"So I say to you: Ask and it will be given to you; seek and you will find; knock and the door will be opened to you. For everyone who asks receives; the one who seeks finds; and to the one who knocks, the door will be opened. "Which of you fathers, if your son asks for a fish, will give him a snake instead? Or if he asks for an egg, will give him a scorpion? If you then, though you are evil, know how to give good gifts to your children, how much more will your Father in heaven give the Holy Spirit to those who ask him!"
-Jesus Christ (Luke 11:9-3)

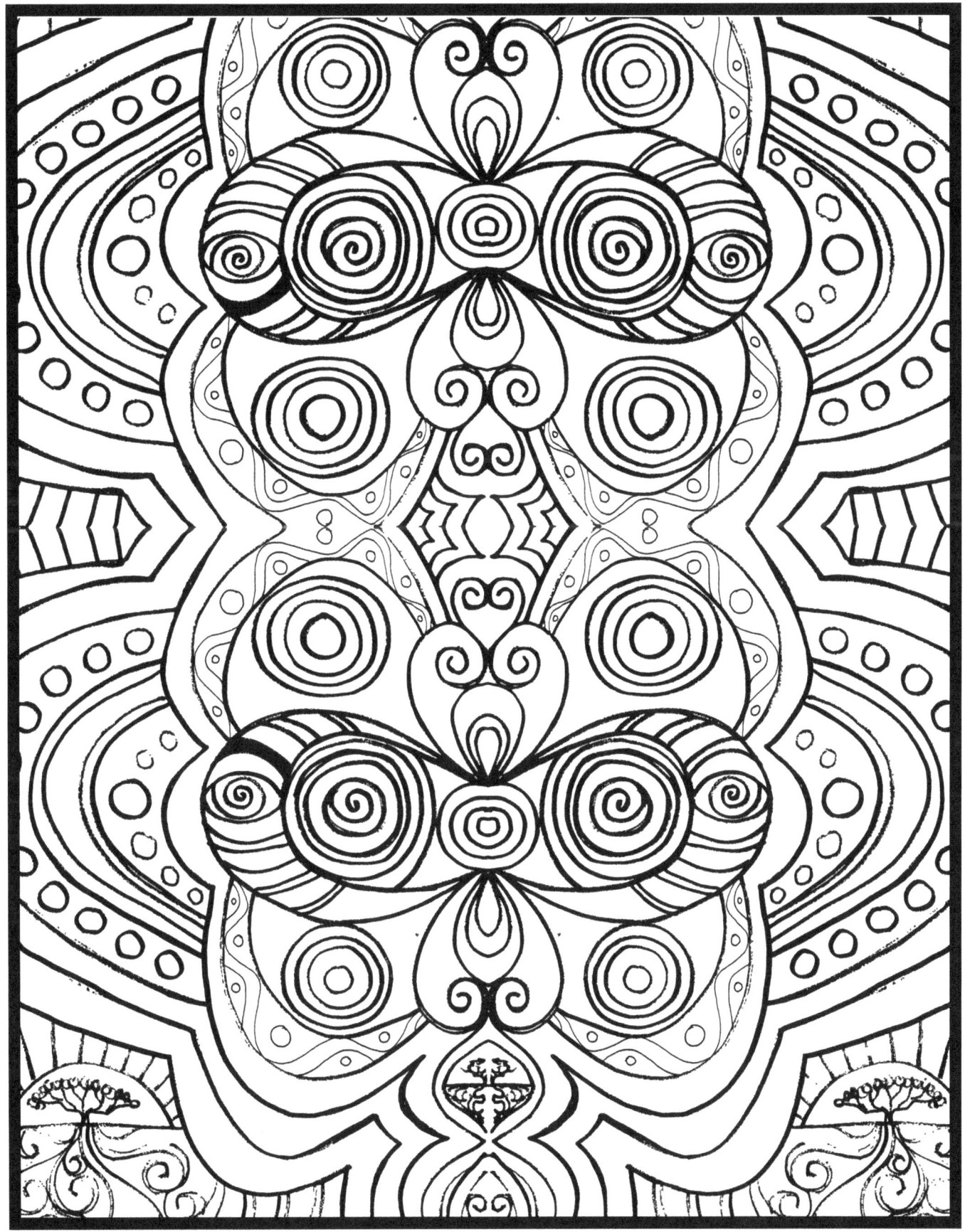

Sending My Prayers:

_____   _____

_____   _____

_____   _____

_____   _____

_____   _____

_____   _____

_____   _____

_____   _____

_____   _____

_____   _____

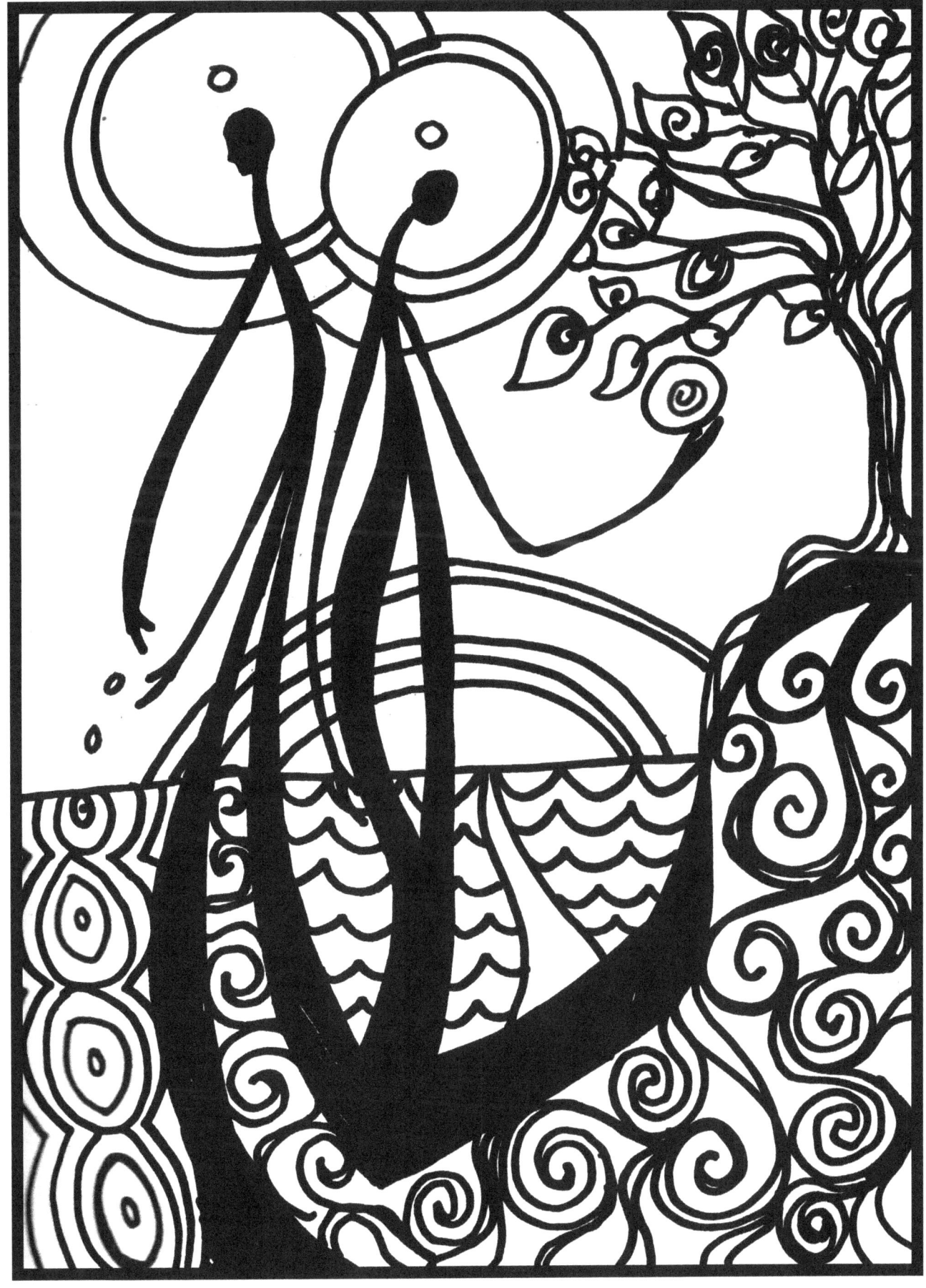

Dreams From Above The Firmament

Tree of life grows
in a sound mind,
beauty of correct thinking,
visions revealed in dreams.

The beloved Holy Spirit
inspires good meditations,
renewing the soul with clean waters,
pouring out love and wisdom.

With an universe of grace
and an unconquerable love
vibrations of future memories
given to gifted prophecies.

Symbols and signs interpreted
seen with a single eye
gifted from the Most High
to the sound mind.

-nathanjtaylor

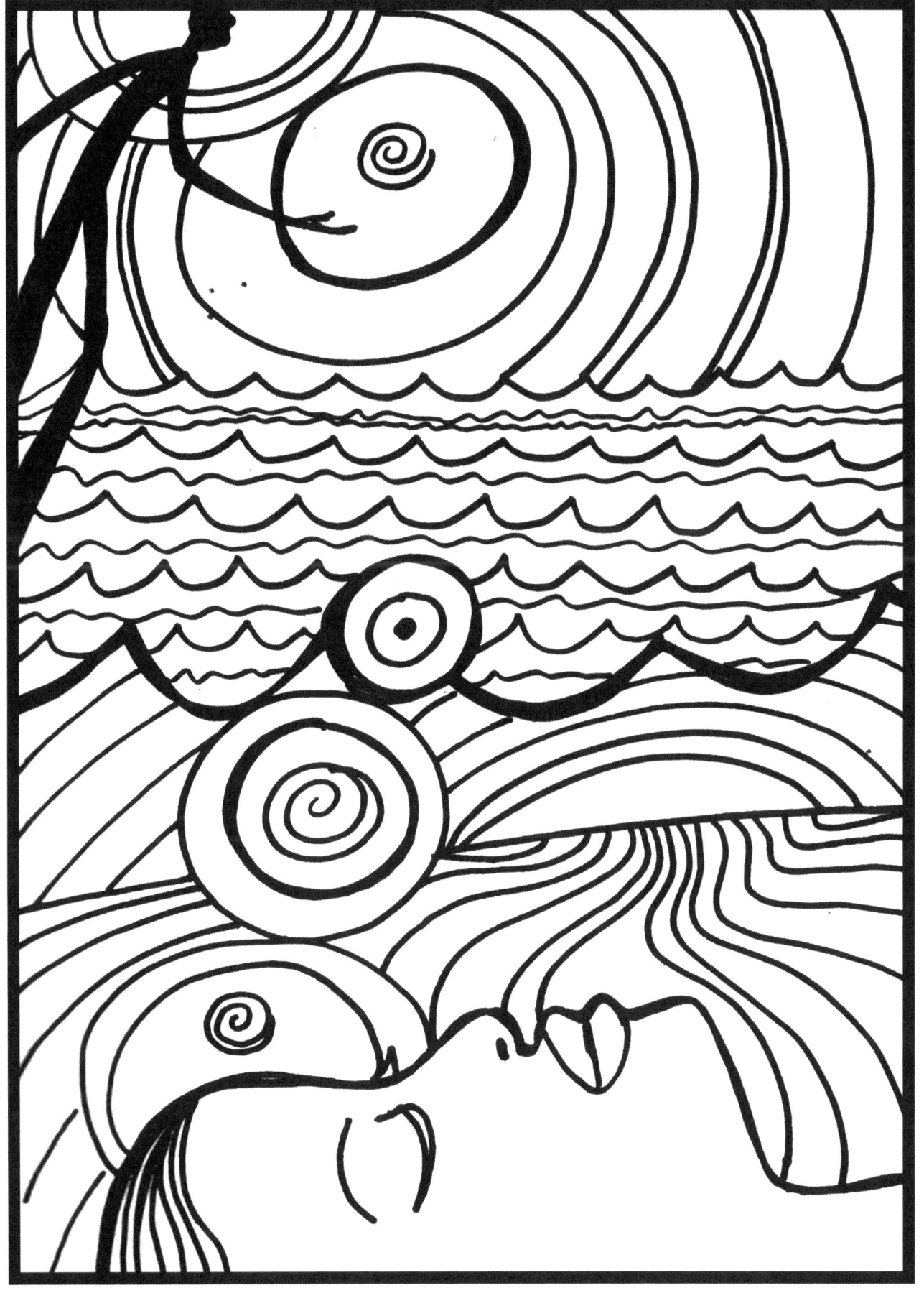

Seven Laws Of Manifestation
Fundamental Keys Of Achieving Goals

1 **Pray:** Connect with the Most High, the force of creation with positive affirmation and gratitude for inspiration and guidance.

2 **Daydream:** Allow yourself to freely dream of the future you want, everything begins in the mind.

3 **Write:** Very important step to write down ideas and goals, increase the power of visualization with drawings, photos, or prototypes.

4 **Research:** Learn as much as you can about your desired goal, the internet and books are great tools.

5 **Plan:** Starting from the end write a step-by-step plan of how to reach your desired goals.

6 **Action:** Step-by-step, execute your plan with action from the beginning and in the proper order.

7 **Persist:** Continue and repeat the process, you will have set backs and failures. You may take a break, or adapt your goals, but never give up!

7 Spiritual Works Of Good

1. To instruct the ignorant.
2. To counsel the doubtful.
3. To admonish sinners.
4. To bear wrongs patiently.
5. To forgive offences willingly.
6. To comfort the afflicted.
7. To pray for the living and the dead

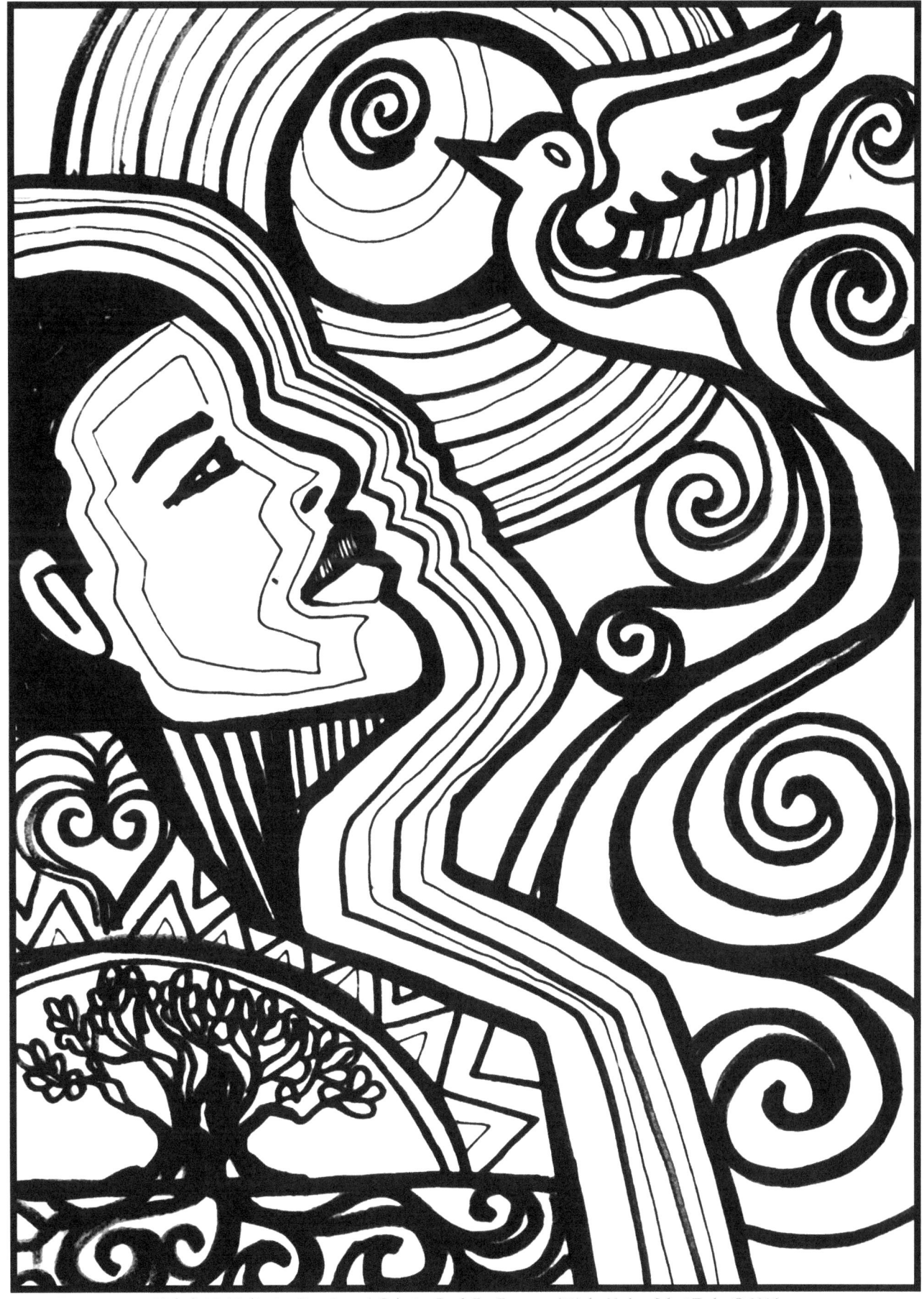

"The gift of mental power comes from God, Divine Being, and if we concentrate our minds on that truth, we become in tune with this great power. My Mother had taught me to seek all truth in the Bible."

-Nikola Tesla

"There are many ways in which people aremade aware of their power to believe in the supremacy of Divine guidance and power: through music or visual art, some event or experience decisively influencing their life, looking through a microscope or telescope, or just by looking at the miraculous manifestations or purposefulness of Nature."

— Ernst B. Chain, winner of the Nobel Prize in Medicine and Physiology for the discovery of penicillin.

"I believe in God. In fact, I believe in a personal God who acts in and interacts with the creation. I believe that the observations about the orderliness of the physical universe, and the apparently exceptional fine-tuning of the conditions of the universe for the development of life suggest that an intelligent Creator is responsible."

—William D. Phillips, Nobel Prize Winner in Physics for development of methods to cool and trap atoms with laser light.

"The ghostly presence of virtual particles defies rational common sense and is non-intuitive for those unacquainted with physics. Religious belief in God, and Christian belief that God became Man around two thousand years ago, may seem strange to common-sense thinking. But when the most elementary physical things behave in this way, we should be prepared to accept that the deepest aspects of our existence go beyond our common-sense intuitions."

*–**Tony Hewish, Nobel Prize winning physicist**, quote from the book: Questions of Truth: Fifty-one Responses to Questions about God, Science, and Belief.*

"The more I work with the powers of Nature, the more I feel God's benevolence to man; the closer I am to the great truth that everything is dependent on the Eternal Creator and Sustainer; the more I feel that the so-called science, I am occupied with, is nothing but an expression of the Supreme Will, which aims at bringing people closer to each other in order to help them better understand and improve themselves. I am proud to be a Christian. I believe not only as a Christian, but as a scientist as well. A wireless device can deliver a message through the wilderness. In prayer the human spirit can send invisible waves to eternity, waves that achieve their goal in front of God."

- Guglielmo Marconi (Electrical engineer, Noble Prize winner, inventor of wireless radio)

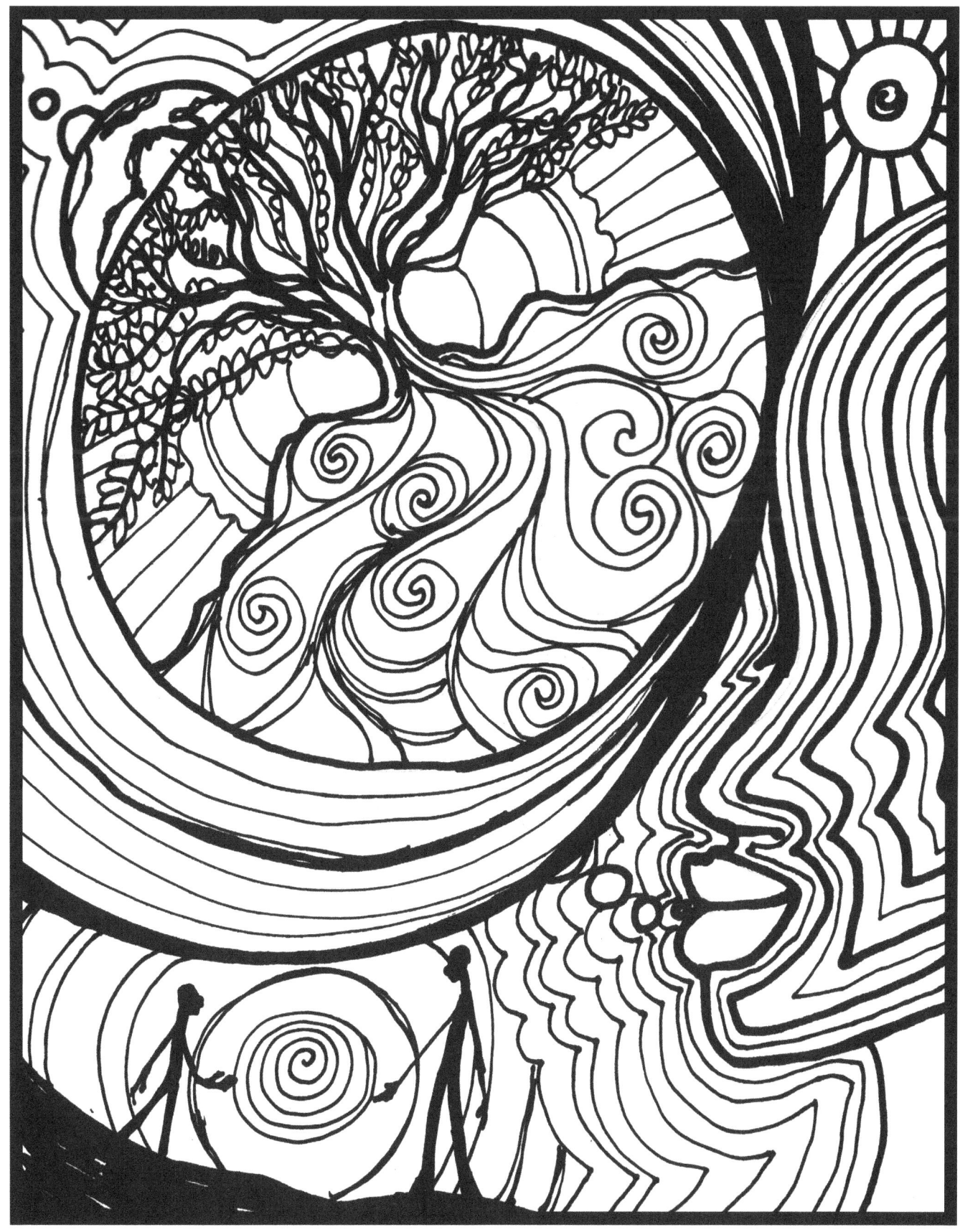

I'm Grateful For:

_____   _____

_____   _____

_____   _____

_____   _____

_____   _____

_____   _____

_____   _____

_____   _____

_____   _____

_____   _____

Holy Spirit Meditation Drawings: A Coloring Book For Everyone (#1) by Nathan Jalani Taylor © 2016

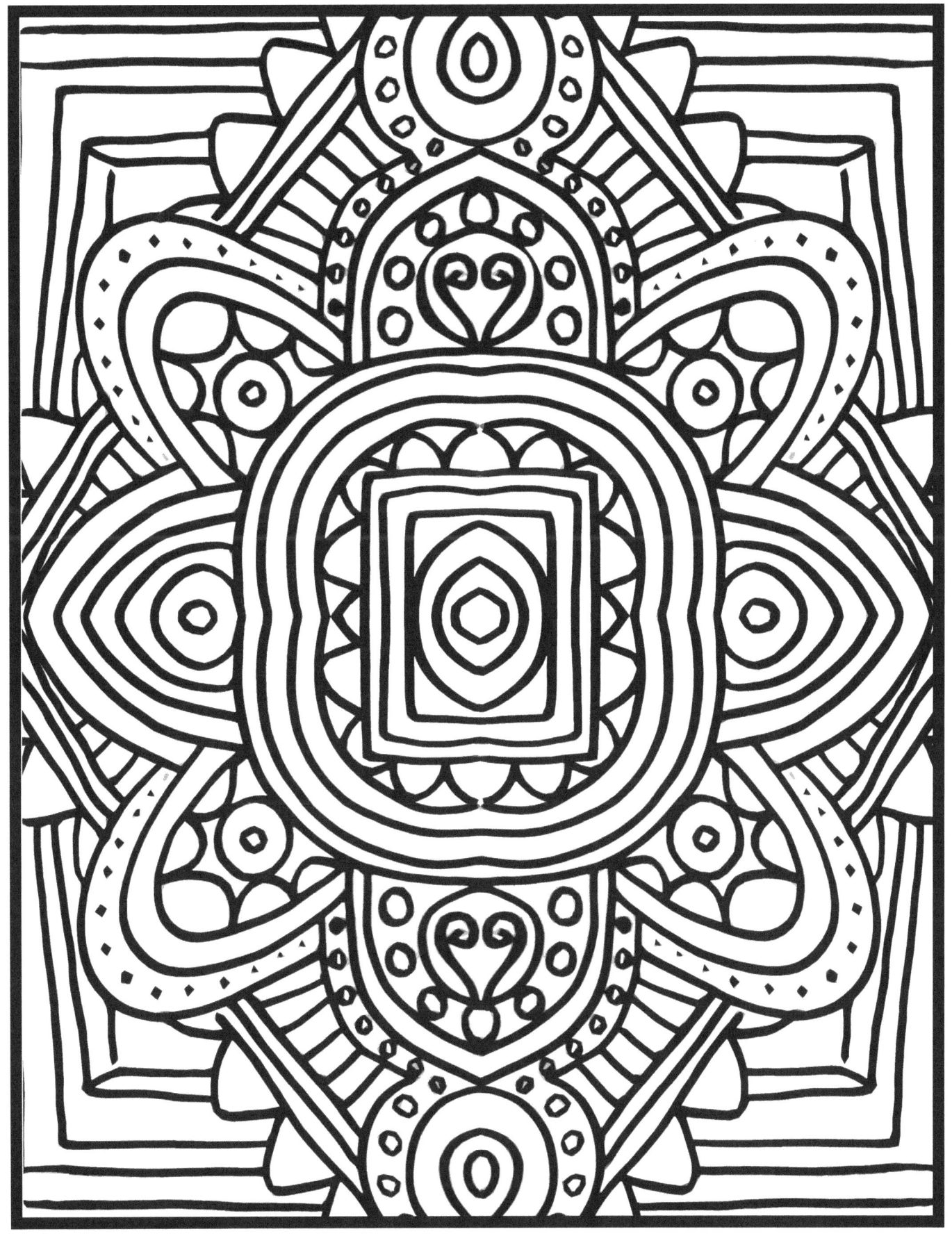

"Prayer Walker." Spread Love and Good Vibes. Planting seeds of faith. Connecting to your roots. Bearing good fruit. Bless your heart. Bless your home. Bless your hood. Bless your nation. Bless your world. In the power of the Holy Spirit. In Jesus name. Amen.

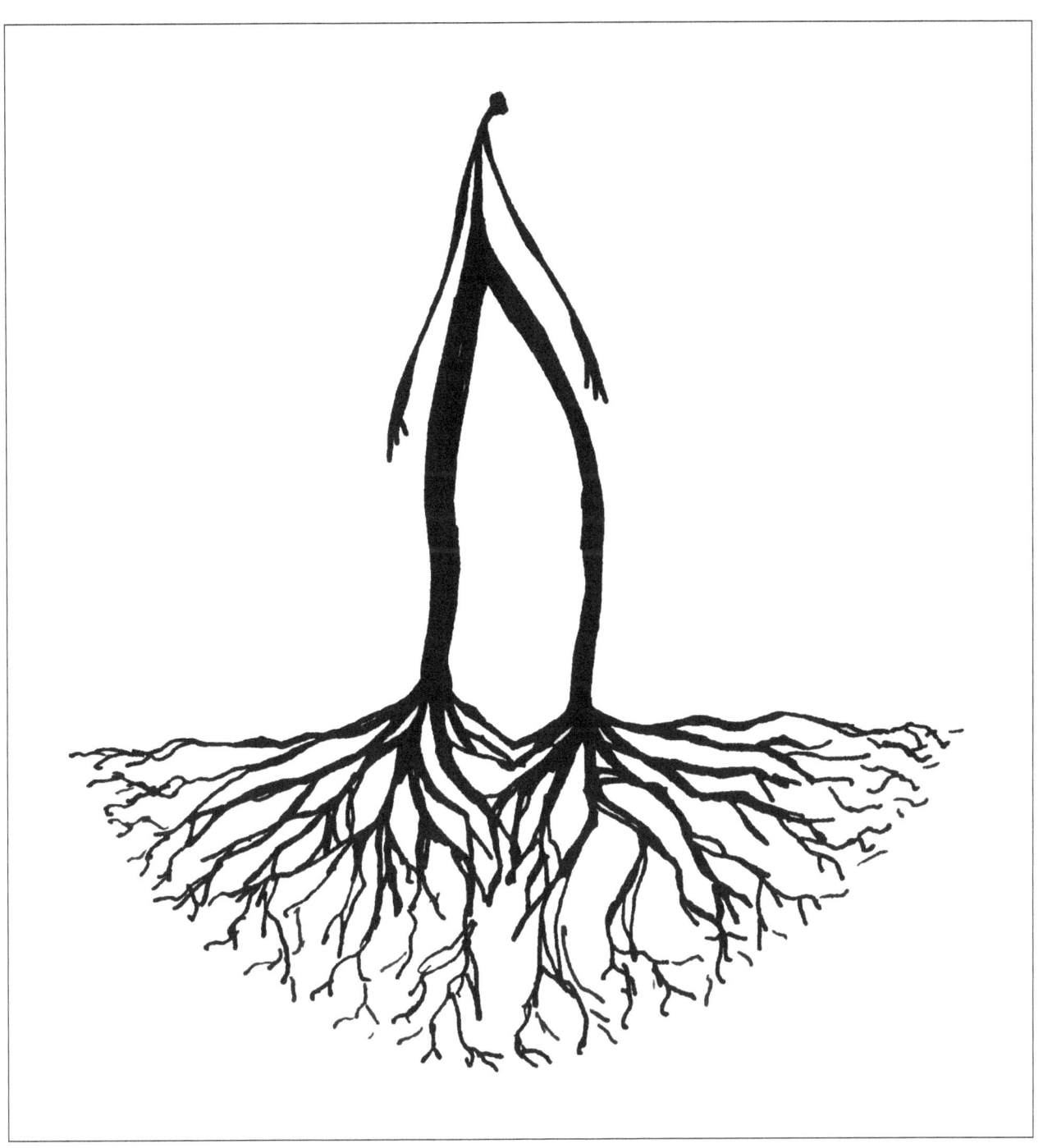

Dedicated to my family & friends.
Thank you for your continued support.
-Nathan Jalani Taylor

www.ingramcontent.com/pod-product-compliance
Lightning Source LLC
Chambersburg PA
CBHW041921180526
45172CB00013B/1354